Published by Ideals Publishing Corporation
Nashville, Tennessee 37214

Printed and bound in Belgium.

ISBN 0-8249-8616-4

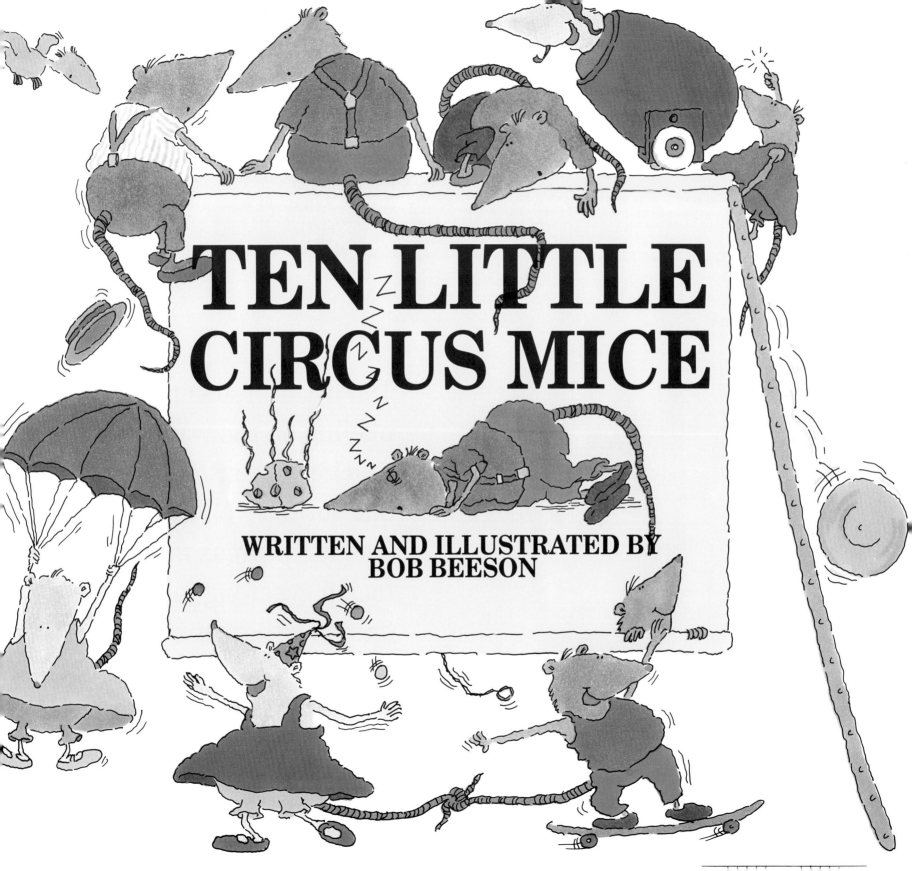

TEN LITTLE CIRCUS MICE

WRITTEN AND ILLUSTRATED BY
BOB BEESON

Ten little circus mice
playing on the wall;
practiced their bigtop acts—
but not too well at all.
One little circus mouse
took a great big fall,
and now there are
nine little circus mice
playing on the wall.

Nine little circus mice
playing on the wall;
one tried to juggle
brightly colored balls.
This little circus mouse
took a great big fall,
and now there are
eight little circus mice
playing on the wall.

Eight little circus mice
playing on the wall;
one wobbled on a cycle
just a tad too tall.
This little circus mouse
took a great big fall,
and now there are
seven little circus mice
playing on the wall.

Seven little circus mice
playing on the wall;
one balanced in the air
on his nose so small.
This little circus mouse
took a great big fall,
and now there are
six little circus mice
playing on the wall.

Six little circus mice
playing on the wall;
one shot into the air
like a rodent cannonball.
This little circus mouse
took a great big fall,
and now there are
five little circus mice
playing on the wall.

BOOM!

Five little circus mice
playing on the wall;
one lost his balance
and his favorite rubber ball.
This little circus mouse
took a great big fall,
and now there are
four little circus mice
playing on the wall.

Four little circus mice
playing on the wall;
one stood in a place
that wasn't safe at all.
This little circus mouse
took a great big fall,
and now there are
three little circus mice
playing on the wall.

Three little circus mice
playing on the wall;
one wore a new red dress
and looked just like a doll.
This little circus mouse
took a great big fall,
and now there are
two little circus mice
playing on the wall.

Two little circus mice
playing on the wall;
one walked a tightrope
that made her look so tall.
This little circus mouse
took a great big fall,
and now there is
one little circus mouse
playing on the wall.

One little circus mouse
playing on the wall;
all her friends were gone
and she felt alone and small.
This little circus mouse
took a great big fall,
and now there are
no little circus mice
playing on the wall.

But this little circus mouse
was not alone at all;
as she floated down she heard
her friends begin to call.
This little circus mouse
reached the end of her fall,
and now there are
ten little circus mice
at the bottom of the wall.